I0559212

SUNRISE OF THE SOUL

Inspirational Moments To Light Up Your Life

DARLEEN MILLER

Copyright © 2025
by Darleen Miller

All rights reserved. No portion of this
book may be reproduced in any form
without written permission from the
publisher or author, except as permitted
by U.S. copyright law.

eBook: 978-1-969466-03-8
Paperback: 978-1-969466-04-5
Hardcover: 978-1-969466-05-2

LCCN: 2025918338

Mara Cleveland- Editorial Assistant.

Dedication

Every moment in time has been my
teacher in the exquisite beauty of my
life through all the people, travels,
places, family and friends. I have
shared magical moments of the
heart. I smile knowing that
each day has been a magnificent
gift in the changing colors in this
rainbow of life.

I lift my lamp to a cherished
community that I have known and
loved. All of us shine together
in the light filled moments in the
eyes of love.

<u>Introduction</u>

Several weeks had passed after moving into a new apt. and I recall one early November morning before Mother Nature awakened, I smiled as the aroma of freshly brewed coffee called my name. I sat in front of my east facing window awaiting the first glimpse of a new late fall morning. On that day, the skies began to vibrate with an energy that mesmerized my mind.

Automatically tears rolled down my cheeks and at that moment I felt a new warmth inside my heart creating a deep gratefulness to be alive and present at that breathtaking moment in time. It was the dawn of an awakening for the soul of humanity.

Each day WE can breathe and create a light of love for each one of us on our dear planet. Right here, right now, WE need to stop and smell the roses.

"WE"
In 2017, the creation of WISDOM
EVOLUTION was designed to form a
community of like-minded, positive
thinking people. WE believe in
nurturing and fostering a personal and
mutual respect and loving kindness for
the good of all humanity.

The "W" emphasizes our WISDOM.

The "E" supports the EVOLUTION of
an expanded philosophy
of the motto—

TOGETHER WE RISE.

TOGETHER WE RISE

Be grateful for every
minute of every day.
That feeling is
ESSENTIAL for change.

CHANGE is inevitable.
Through our feelings
and thoughts,
WE
can recognize TRUTH.

I am the center
of my own universe
which creates
my own realities

Be open
and accepting
to the
moments in life.
Let them
float and flow
in the
light of love.

Humanity
needs the
unifying energy
of LOVE.

Find the
sweetness in
life no matter
the circumstances.
There is always
two sides to
every choice
that is made.

Love and
compassion will
shift the energy
all the days of
our lives.

Gentle smile,
Breathe and
relax your shoulders
as often as
you can each day.
Your body
will be grateful.

In this moment,
know the
TRUTH of LOVE
and UNITY for
ALL humankind.

The Powerful Shift
in Energy
on the Planet
lies within
the hearts of all.

The thinking mind
is driven
by feelings.

REMEMBER!
Each of us
has a journey
in this lifetime.
Explore
ALL possibilities.

Believe
and
celebrate
the power in
FORGIVENESS.

A change
of heart
can change
a life.

Anger and fear
limit
our experience
of
LOVE and JOY.

WE
are connecting
heart to heart
in an
evolution
of change.

WE
must rest in the
calming energy
of PEACE
and
HARMONY.

LET GO
OF FEAR.
Breathe
the precious
light of the
soul.

Together
WE
become
ONE voice
for peace
and
compassion.

The heart knows--
The brain
interprets
the rule of life.

Recognize
CHANGE in life.
Create a new
reason to celebrate
every SUNRISE.

When WE
share our stories,
WE Rise
to
new heights
of
inner beauty.

Now is the hour to
EVOLVE
with a new
light-filled
Wisdom
of
joyfulness.

Respect for
one another
is found
in the energies
of our
differences.

When WE
change our
mind and actions
in life, the
OUTCOME
will change.

Be STILL
and feel
the radiance
of love.

THE RISE
OF
HUMANITY
is rising in light.
SMILE and
LIVE! LOVE!

Live life
to the
fullest knowing
WE
are an
expression of love.

In the
quiet moments
of life,
discover
your truth.

Treasure
every moment
in your life
with love.

The brain
interprets the
exquisite Wisdom
of the heart.

Live
with a
new attitude
of life
ON purpose.

If you
light a lamp
for others,
it will also
brighten your path.

With every
conscious breath,
WE
evolve in
LIGHT.

Find the
quiet time
every day.
It's a
HEALING moment.

The quieter
you become,
the more
you can hear.

Engage the
heart and
the mind
to create
BALANCE.

The elevator
of life is
ascending
to limitless
heights.
Going UP??

EVERYTHING
emits energy--
our thoughts
create
the outcome.

CHOOSE
to live a life
of TRUTH
and
INTEGRITY.
Your heart will
be grateful.

When WE
encounter fears
in life, the chemistry
and immune systems
are compromised.
Be open to
your light, NOW.

Be a
pioneer
in the
ministry of
light and
create a
community
of joy.

In this
moment
in time,
let us
KNOW that
TOGETHER
WE
RISE.

Know the
answers
in life
are
always within.

The Wisdom
of how
WE
handle change
lies within
our choices.

Compassion
and Love
are the
cornerstones
of a
peaceful life.

Each day
WE
can choose
to build a bridge
to a
higher reality.

Listen
to life's
messages with a
loving heart.

This moment
in time
is the
most important
one in life.
Be in present
time awareness.

When
WE
know true love,
WE
are free of fear.

At this moment
in time, trust
WE are exactly
where WE need
to be.

One of the greatest
gifts in life
is the discovery
of who
WE really are.

Be fully
present in life--
Appreciate
everyone and
everything.
The message
WILL evolve.

Breathe!
The Heartbeat
of all life
goes on and on...

Love, Light
and
Compassion
are the
answers to all
of our fatigue.

Shadows in
our lives create
anger and fear.
Seek the light
of the soul.

To know
the messages
of the
heart wisdom
is to
walk a path
in LIGHT.

WE
are here
to change
the world one
thought at a time.

True friendship
evolves when
the silence between
2 people
is comfortable.

The soft, loving
feminine energy
is growing
in our lives.
FEEL IT!

Daily WE
create and
recognize the
DIVINE light
of the heart by
knowing
WE are Love.

As
WE
live in the
awareness of the
heart light, there will
not be reason to
live in fear, darkness,
hate and anger.

There is great
wisdom in the
light-filled cells
in the body.
TRUST
and
Live Love

Enjoy
every moment
of the dream
your heart makes.

Let us
HONOR
and
CELEBRATE
the gentle feminine
energy of the
Divine Mother.
It lives in the message
of the heart.

If WE
encounter obstacles
in life, perhaps
they are the path
WE need to take.

The
essence of life is
CONSTANT
CHANGE.
It cannot be stopped.

No matter who
tells us what
WE
should or should not
do in life, the final
decision lies within
our own conscious
awareness.

WE
are a part
of all life,
WE are the unity that
is right
in front of us.

WE
Cocreate
our realities with the
soul of humanity.

Breathe in--
see the
light of creation.
Exhale and say;
"I am LOVE".

It is time
to join hands
energetically
and
move onward
and
upward.

Until
WE
know for sure,
ask the self,
Who AM I?
Why AM I here?

Change your
mind and actions,
and life
WILL change.

Focus
on compassion
of the heart energy.
It's about LOVE.

Light
creates a pathway
of information from
the Heart of God.

The connection
to a Joyful life
is found in the
Wisdom of
the Heart.

Every day
in every way
WE
are shaped by
our feelings and
our thoughts.
FEEL LOVE

There will
always be
a moment in life
when you
KNOW you have
something
meaningful to share.

When
WE believe
WE
are reflections
of Divine Light,
the World
will change.

The world
has doorways
to open.
Await the miracles.

ALL
is possible when
WE
see one another
in the
LIGHT OF LOVE.

CHANGE
is a
constant in life.
On that you can trust.

If the days
and nights
seem dark,
LIGHT A CANDLE.

Every day
in every way,
WE can evolve with an
attitude of compassion
for ALL humanity.

Each
of us is the
CENTER
of our own
LIGHT FORCE.

The answer
to all questions
evolves in the
quiet wisdom
of the heart.

Be gentle
with thoughts
and actions as
WE
live each day in the
light of love.

Allow change
to be
your teacher--
not your enemy.

Create
harmony every day
of your life.
The energy
will CHANGE.

In every
situation, choose
to act first
and react later.

Sing a lullaby
of love for the
planet and
notice a new light
of connection
with the world.

Let go
of rigid schedules
and BREATHE
in the quiet
energy of love.

Breathe
in the gentle
Light of the heart.
Know Love.

A new
definition for
CHANGE OF LIFE--
evolution of a new
Heart and loving
consciousness.

The shift
in power on the
planet lies within
the heart of civilization.

Love
is the foundation of
every choice--
FEEL IT!
KNOW IT!
BE IT!

ALL lives
are sacred in the
gentle expression
of the heart.

Breathe in and
realize that you
are HERE and it is
NOW--SMILE
and exhale.

Energy is evolving
both personally
and globally.
NOW is the time
to create a new
CELEBRATION OF LIFE.

Our lives
were not built in a day.
All of our yesterday's
have brought us
gracefully in today.
Tomorrow will take
care of itself.

Together
WE
can explore our gifts
and talents for a
Peaceful World.

Find time
every day
to be STILL and
QUIET the mind.

For one
moment every day,
focus on a happy
experience. It will
always change
your energy.

Our feelings
and thoughts can
CHANGE
the energy
of the world.

Replace
negativity with feelings
of acceptance
and
Loving Kindness.

WE
can choose to explore
the FEMININE Energy
creating a KINDER,
bigger picture of
COMPASSION.

Believe
in the magic
and
wonder every day
in every way.

Allow change
to happen in your life.
It is the constant fact
WE
can trust.

Create time
to recognize
the beauty
in all life.

Each of us
MUST
take charge of our
planetary healing.
WE
create and become the
NEW FRONTIER.

Choose to deep
breathe several times
during the day. A happy
heart
depends on it.

Listen
to the
quiet message
of the heart.

WE
are the center of
our own Universe.
Create from LOVE.

When WE
share the light of the
heart, the dark night
of the soul disappears.
BE the light you wish to
find in the world.

The idea of living begins in the heart. The brain is the interpreter.

At every crossroad,
WE
can choose
the foundation of love.

All events
are happening
at the right place
at the right time.

For a moment
each morning,
breathe in the
energy of love.

Every day
in every way,
WE
can contribute
to a Peaceful World.

This present
moment in time
is precious.
Take it to heart.

WE
are born to
live life as
WE
choose.

Together
WE
are experiencing a
NEW AWAKENING.

As new
energy evolves for all of
us, it is time
to create a NEW
Celebration of Life.

Change your mind;
Change your life.

Every choice
WE
make in life
ultimately belongs
to each of us.
OWN IT!!

In the silence,
WE
can listen to the
message of the heart.

Keep the mind,
body and spirit
in good health.

LIFE IS WHAT
WE MAKE IT!

When WE
Change our feelings
and thoughts about life,
WE
WILL awaken a new
energy of success!

Breathe in LOVE!
Breathe out fear!

Knowing begins
in the energy
of the heart--
acting is the function of
the brain.

Together
WE
Rise in the light
for humanity.

Have FAITH!
We are on the
path of LOVE.

Every day
in every way,
WE can choose
to enjoy life.

Connect to
your own light--
it will guide
your way.

Each day
with love,
WE can create a life
ON PURPOSE.

Change your mind
about life and
notice the energy
of the heart.
Release FEAR--create
a new connection to
your heart light.

WE
are divinely connected
in a loving energy.

FAITH
has
NO LIMITS.

In
the silence,
the light of love
glows anew.

There
is no ending or
beginning to energy.
It just IS.

WE
can rise to the
experience of our
own dreams
by
knowing the truth
in every sunrise.

Embrace
the energy
of Divine Inspiration.
BE THE JOYFUL
LIGHT of LOVE.

Every day,
in every way
WE
can feel deep
connections to a
beautiful life.

Find
TRUTH
and
BALANCE
in life.

WE
are building bridges
to a Higher Reality.

Together
WE
create a
POWERFUL
light force.

How
WE
live life
is our message
to the world.

Lighten UP!!
Find time
to laugh
and
enjoy life.

Be renewed
in the light of
loving compassion.

Sing a lullaby of love for
the survival
of our planet.

Living in the
light of love,
WE
are divinely
connected.

Radiate a message
of Love for ALL.

Let us
move forward
in the feminine
energy of the heart.

Breathe
in the quiet gentle
expression of your life.

WE
cannot prevent
the Passage of Time.

WE
are the Caregivers
of LIGHT.

BE KIND
to yourself
and to all of life.

Let go
and
know the
power in your light.

With Love,
ALL things
are possible.

The Center
of our own universe
lies within
our conscious
awareness.

Every day--
create a
moment
of joy in your life.

When
WE live
in the light
of the heart,
WE
create a joyfulness
about life.

Breathe
in--Relax your
shoulders and
BE at Peace.

Breathe in
the LIGHT
of creation.

Change
is constant
evolving energy.

Be renewed
in the choices
WE
make.

WE
perceive our realities
through our senses.
They live with us
through our feelings
and our thoughts.

It's time
to rise to our
heart energies.
TOGETHER WE RISE.

Relax your
shoulders as
you breathe.
Feel that moment
of peace.

When WE
remove the blinders
from the brain
with truth as our focus,
WE can open new
doorways of light.

WE
feel happy when
WE
listen to the message
of the heart.

If WE
are alive,
WE have Purpose.

Live Life
with a loving light
of the heart.

Sing the song
your heart
was meant to sing.

Loving
feelings enhance
our vitality as well as
our reality.

Love the self
with compassion
in every choice
that is made.

When
WE
think and act
the same way
WE
have always lived,
nothing will change.

When
WE
feel our own sense
of value,
Everything
shifts into LIGHT.

Today-- I am
uplifted by the
BEAUTY in Nature.

The
Divine Feminine energy
is growing from HEART
to BRAIN.

FEEL
AND
KNOW.

The world
is our classroom...
Learning the lessons
takes time.

LOVE
is creating
kindness in life.

Together
WE
must let go of fear
and listen to the
voice of the heart.

When
WE
change the epidemic of
fear and anger
to love, the light of
the heart will shine.

There is no
time like
the present to do
what is RIGHT.

The survival
of humanity depends
on an evolving
civilization.

In every day,
in every way,
know the
gentle light of love.

It is time
to find your
mission in life.
What others
think of us
is NONE
of our business.

Let go of fear!
Float and Flow
in Love!

HOW are
WE
contributing to
PEACE in our world?

Be the
JOY
you wish to find
in the world.

Be comforted
in the
new awareness of
your life.

Cherish your family.
Choose
Harmony with
one another.

Find
the beauty in
EVERYTHING...
SMILE.

The

essence of

ALL life is ENERGY.

There
is a lesson to learn
in every event in life.
It's how
WE
handle it that makes
the difference.

WE
are divinely
connected in a light of
loving energy.

Every moment
of every day and night,
WE evolve in change.

Be gentle as you
walk a path of joy.

Shadows in our lives
create places of fear.
Seek the light of
your heart.

Choose to deep
breathe several times
during the day.
A happy heart depends
on it.

As our energy evolves, WE all create a new celebration of life.

Every day in every way, believe in the magic of a sunrise.

Time for the Phoenix to rise from the ashes of fear, anger and hate.

BE THE LIGHT YOU WISH TO FIND IN THE WORLD.

About The Author

Growing up in a war-torn world, I recall the many steamy hours during the summer days and nights in Washington, DC. I would sit on a porch swing daydreaming about my future. I asked myself repeatedly —"Who am I?" and "Why am I here?".

Sundays were set aside for church services that included Sunday School, morning and evening services. I realized all of it taught me to be devoted to a God Presence that was nowhere and everywhere at the same time. As I reflect now, the hours of religious education eventually led me to a rich understanding of my connection to an energy larger than life itself.

I always enjoyed my daily participation in school because it challenged my mind to explore the many aspects of learning about life. This included participating in sports, music, and all the academic subjects which helped me explore every level of my education.

It was my joy to write special messages to family and friends on various celebrations. These were the foundational moments that prompted the book creation of "YES! IT REALLY IS ALL ABOUT ME: The Journey of a Lifetime". This book was dedicated to the caregivers of the world. It suggested a new personal understanding to love and nurturing the mind, body and soul.

In 2017, with the creation of WISDOM EVOLUTION, I encouraged everyone to lift their awareness to include a clearer vision of life, in a stressful world.

Recently, as I moved to my new home, I found a large container filled with many notebooks of my creative writing. I was able to catch glimpse of a new perspective about life and inspiration to open windows and attitudes toward a purposeful life. It is never too late to recognize that the *heartbeat of life goes on and on...*

Enjoy my labor of love, SUNRISE OF THE SOUL. IT will light up your life.

Heartfully yours, Darleen

www.ingramcontent.com/pod-product-compliance
Lightning Source LLC
Chambersburg PA
CBHW051306120626
46547CB00015B/2116